Love verses Hate

JAMES "MR. SPEAKER" SEARS

LOVE VERSES HATE

Copyright © 2025 James "Mr. Speaker" Sears Jr.

ISBN (Paperback): 979-8-89672-047-8
ISBN (Hardback): 979-8-89672-048-5
ISBN (Ebook): 979-8-89672-049-2

Printed in the United States of America.

PROMINENT
BOOKS

5830 E 2nd St, Ste 7000 #9983
Casper, WY 82609
USA

Dedication

This is dedicated to those still searching for love, to love's lost, love's damaged, love's mistreated, and to love not returned. This is dedicated to love's pain, love's happiness, and to the greatness of love. May love shine on us all!

Contents

Chapter I : All About Love 7
How to deal? 9
The Greatest 10
Tall, Dark, and Handsome 12
My Ride or Die Chick 13
Yin and Yang 14
Soul Food Loving (To all the great cooks in the world) 16
Stop and Stare 18
Forgive Me 19
Expiration 20
Beauty is a Beast 22
Love Versus Hate 25

Chapter II: Some Kind of Hate 27
The Warning Shot 29
Who are you? 30
What have you done for me? 31
So 32
Snap If You Know This Woman 34
Tell Them To STOP 36
Something Just Is Not Right 38
Bitter B's 40
Sexual Death 42

Chapter III: Sensually Speaking 43
SHE 45
The Best Ever 47
Pre-Sex 51
Bed Hustler 54
After Sex 56
Sex Education 58
Verbal Lap Dance 60
New Foreplay 62

Poetry Prostitution 64
You   I want to haiku you 65
Sexy Woman 66

Chapter IV: Women I Have Loved ... 67
Unseen Romance 69
Second 70
My Queen 71
Hello Again 72
A Note to the "I" 73
Team Sears 74
The "I" Has It 75
Apple Pie 76
Vessel 77
Early Morning Come Back 78

Chapter V: Biblical Love 79
Biblical Love Poem 81
Love Story 84
A Good Thing 86
Forgive 88

Chapter VI: Love Wins 89
Love or Hate? 91
Rumble! (Trust vs. Love) 92
Love Talk 94
The Language of Respect 96
Battle Buddy 98
Relationship Table 99
Decision 100
All Meat and No Potatoes 102
Lover's Prayer 104

Acknowledgments 107

CHAPTER I
All About Love

How to deal?

Would someone tell grown men how to deal with broken hearts, please? Who knew the result of love would bring these giants to their knees? For men, there are no support groups or midnight therapy sessions. It seems a broken heart is just one of life's cruel lessons. Someone please, write a book, give a class, but help these men right now. I am trying to prevent you ladies from getting caught up as he rebounds. Contrary to popular belief, men suffer just like you, but our male friends do not want to hear this and they really do not know what to say or do. Love comes and love goes, love lives and love dies, we're hurt deep inside because most men were never taught or learned how to really cry. See, lifting weights or taking medications just does not freaking work.

Someone really should have told men how much a broken heart hurts. I messed around and got caught up in something I cannot fix. I got played and now, I am standing here looking stupid and feeling sick. Car troubles, get a mechanic. Need home repairs?

A carpenter can handle that with a bank debit.

A doctor can fix your broken arm, there are even fixes for your jacked-up credit. This pain in my heart is bursting right through my chest.

Where is my easy button to fix this, so I can get some rest?

Yes, I have heard, "Time heals all wounds," so they say. But I've also heard people carried broken hearts right to their very graves.

Well, I don't have the answers. No instant solutions nor magic potions.

Both male and female hearts are fragile and easily broken. Now I know where doggish men come from, the ones that make ladies cringe.

They are the products of broken hearts, out hurting women for kicks or revenge.

Now my therapy is jazz, blues, and sad country-and-western songs.

I listen to this music like medication until the pain in my heart is gone.

I tried, I failed, and just like in baseball, I swung at love and missed!

So today, I stand here, still searching for my last first kiss!

The Greatest

Simply the most powerful utterance ever heard.
It is difficult to describe with just written or spoken word.
While birds and bees do sing in the trees
this powerful word can bring anyone to his or her knees.

I am talking about the love that flows from a man's heart.
The kind of love that gave this world its jump-start.
The kind of love that can make you walk twenty-plus miles
Yes, the kind of love a parent has for his or her child.

Faith can move mountains while hope springs eternal;
but love is greater than both of them, so record that in your mental journals.
Love can cause you to help a person, whom you may not even know.
Love can give you comfort when you are completely out of dough.

Love was present in the beginning, yes at the creation
and love will be there at the fall of the last nation.
Love conquers all no matter what fight you are in.
If love is your weapon, then you will definitely win.

Love is universal as it can be spoken in any tongue:
In **Spanish** you are mi vita, which means you are **My Life**.
In **Italian** you are ti amo mi amorita, which means **I Love You My Love**.
In **Arabic** you are I aynav which means, you are **My Eyes**.
In **German** you are mein schatz, which means you are **My Treasure**.
In **Tagalog** from the **Philippines**, you are Mahal Kita, which means, **I Love You**!
In that great **South African** tongue of **Zulu**, you are Ou Uie San Wa som, which means you are **My Love**.
And in the language of love **French**, you are tu es mon unavial which means, **You Are My Universe.**

God is the source of love; remember that when you decide to mate.
Understand, you could be acting like the devil when you show hate.

Beauty and love should not be mixed together
beauty is superficial; while true love lasts forever.
Do not awaken love until you are truly ready,
    because it comes with a burden that is extremely heavy. *Love* has been known to work
miracles & deep wounds it has healed
but used improperly, love has the power to even kill.

Love has sent Soldiers to war and has guided the lost to safe ground.
Love protects the weak and keeps smiles from becoming frowns.

    Love has been known to save some from a sure death.
It has also caused some to give up all of their wealth.
    Love is not guaranteed to any of us, now that is real
but until you have truly loved, then you have not actually lived.

Love can turn enemies to allies and cause friends to treat you better.
True love always shines no matter what type of weather.
    Love conquers all as it always wins; just give it a try.
Love has billions of victories, no losses, and it has never been tied.

    Love everyone no matter if they are a friend or a foe.
    This does not mean you can't fight for what's right; just don't harbor hate, always let it go.
    There is only one source for this word and that is from above.
So, remember that God is actually pure love!

Tall, Dark, and Handsome

Tall, dark, and handsome, that is what you ladies ask for,
  but for most of my life, zero for three was my score.

I wanted to be tall, so I ate my veggies, but I did not grow.
  Even wanted to be handsome with an afro, but God said no.

I wanted to be darker like most of the people in my hood.
  Laid out in the sun for hours, but that did not do any good.

Well, I am not following the ladies guide for desirable men.
  Heck, most women don't even like the conditions they are in.

Locate the perfect lady, look around, and make it snappy.
  I bet she has at least three body parts with which she is unhappy.

My feet, butt, or thighs are too big and my skin is too light,
  and if you ask her weight, she might just fight.

Tall, dark and handsome, well that is not for me,
  How about I introduce you ladies to some better qualities?

Try faithful, honest, loyal, intelligent, hardworking, and paid;
  anything less could have you searching for an upgrade.

Tall, dark, and handsome. Well baby, that concept is out the door.
  Trust me, a really good man is packing so much more.

My Ride or Die Chick

She is down, no matter what both day and night.
She is always watching my back because we are just that tight.

She is trustworthy and loyal as she is the best kind of friend.
She speaks my love language and always helps me comprehend.

She is patient, kind, loving, and intelligent.
She is giving, honest, dependable, and heaven-sent.

Compassionate, and she always helps if she can.
Her inner strength is twice that of any man.

When I'm down she is two inches lower.
When I'm hurt, she places me on her shoulders.

She is a rider, a roller, and she is my 357-magnum holder.
She my nurse or lawyer, mess with me and she will destroy ya!

She is my right hand and she always understands.
Her heart is as big as the Rio Grande and never lets me crash land.

Her voice is as sweet as music from a baby grand.
If I'm on trial, she is in the witness stand. Keeps me in pocket, from getting out of hand.

Through thick or thin, true friend and she is always there.
You can search a lifetime and never find her anywhere.

And if I ever lost her, I would be completely sick.
See, she is my ride or die chick.

Yin and Yang

You call; I come
You talk; I listen

You quit; I continue
You want; I have

You fall; I lift
You ask; I answer

You look; I find
You lack; I provide

You lose; I recover
You dream; I create

You cry; I comfort
You walk; I run

You fear; I protect
You pour; I drink

You stumble; I balance
You get sick; I play doctor

You point; I go

You throw; I catch
You need; I give

You break; I fix
You attack; I defend

You yell; I smile
You hurt; I heal

You thirst; I quench
You tire; I inspire

You loathe; I love
You itch; I scratch

You sneeze; I bless
You hope; I manifest

You hunger; I feed
You stress; I soothe

You ache; I massage
You are soft; I am hard

Your wish; my command

As your King, I want to be the best man I possibly can.
It is written, "When a man finds a wife, he finds a good thing."

Find is the key word because a good wife cannot be clearly seen,
because the good and bad are stuck together like static cling,
while both are searching for a wedding ring.

See, we are the perfect match as you are my better half!
Yes, better have my dinner on the table, and leave me alone
while I am watching sports on cable.

No seriously, we are no longer individuals so make the transition.
We only have one leader, that is me, so just play your position.

Baby girl, we make a great team like Laura and Steve Urkel,
because just like the Yin and Yang, together we make a perfect circle.

Look, you would be my Queen, the most important person in my life.
I promise to love, honor and protect you every day and with all my might.

That is why I decided to give you my rang, because you are the perfect yin to my yang.

Soul Food Loving (To all the great cooks in the world)

I am trying to be nice because there is no need to be rude
but hands down, the best eating in the world is soul food.

Let me start with the beverages, those refreshing drinks.
The soul food special is sweet tea, then lemonade, or red Kool-Aid, not pink.

The bread is just simply a magnificent feat.
Fried or baked corn bread, hot rolls just taste so sweet.

You must try the sweet potatoes and creamed corn, what wonderful treats.
A highlight are the collard greens with ham hocks, but the meal is not complete.

You'll find green beans, stewed tomatoes, and the best dressing you will ever eat!
And soul food includes baked beans with or without hamburger meat.

My mother's macaroni and cheese is the best, I don't care what you heard!
She should have a sign outside her kitchen that says: "Over 500,000 served!"

Germans eat a lot of pork, that point is not even worth disputa.
But soul food cooks and eats the pig from the roota to the toota.

Soul food prepares pork from chitterlings to pig feet, heck, it even cooks and eats the pig's skin.
Soul food has kept a lot of people from becoming Muslims.

I saw my brother work magic with a turkey one day.
The way he deboned it and then stuffed it, wow, he blew everyone away.

There is another special meat that you should not miss.
You really need to taste how soul food prepares and cooks fish.

Soul food includes turkey, fish, pork and all types of barbeque, there is no doubt, but it is that
barnyard pimp, yes chicken baby, that actually rules the house.

You will never see a stray chicken in my hood, man.
If it takes two steps in the wrong direction, it would end up in a frying pan.

Both my grandmothers were great cooks and that is no lie.
My grandmothers made great desserts and the best being hot apple pies.

You will not find a lot of soul food restaurants while out on a date
because the love that goes into this food is difficult to duplicate.

So, if you want some of the best food, you have just been told.
You can feed the body, but this kind of food nourishes the soul.

Stop and Stare

Girl, you are fine as frog's
hair. Sorry, but I had to stop and stare.

If I could, I would
swear, by your beauty because, you are so fair.

Ask your name if I
dare. Say yes or no, I don't even care,

just want to breathe your air.

Your beauty I
declare, there are few who can compare.

I have looked from Florida to Times
Square. Could not find one anywhere.

Well you should be
Aware: I am adding you to my daily prayers.

Forgive Me

Forgive me, if thinking highly of myself makes you think lowly of me.
Forgive me, if loving me causes you to think less of me. I apologize!
I cannot expect or require you to love me so, I love myself.
I am not saying I am better than you, I am only being the best I can be.
Cannot you see? I am just saying my focus is different.
I am looking up while it appears you are looking directly at me.

  You might see my past, while I see my potential.
  You might be focused on my faults, but I see my improvements.

I've heard the comments "You think you are all of that." Well, the answer is, yes, I do; now tell me, how long have you been able to read minds? Sorry, but I will always think highly of myself.

What I recommend:
Love yourself more while hating others less.
Always look inward before you look outward.
Listen and observe twice as much as you speak.
Keep your opinions of others to yourself, unless you are asked for them.
Seek individuals you can help, you can learn from, and you can love.
Run from those that gossip, lie, and carry a negative spirit.
Be positive and stop judging others.

You will find that it is difficult to move forward while focusing on others.
It's true, it's true, so turn your focus back to you.
At the end of the day, you will realize, it actually takes more strength to be humble, which is extremely wise.

Expiration

Tell me,
why is it that marriage licenses are the only licenses that do not expire?
Could this be why so many homes are burning, but there are no fires?

Look,
let me get right to my many points!
Wedded couples should have to renew their marriage licenses to stay joined.

See,
just because you have been selected,
does not mean your responsibilities should be neglected.

That's why
periodically, your marriage should be inspected,
so bad habits can be detected and hopefully corrected.

Stay connected
as it is your future that would be protected, because your relationship
might be infected.

Both of you could have
been disrespected, with marital wounds that need some disinfectant.

Renewal
of marriage licenses should not be rejected.
Hope, passion, and understanding, into your marriage, could be injected.

*If you are neglecting your responsibilities like providing, cooking, protecting,
or cleaning, then you need your marriage license suspended.*

*If you are sleeping around with other individuals and neglecting your spouse,
then you need your marital privileges revoked and not extended.*

If you do not have nice things to say about your spouse,
then you should be placed on matrimonial probation.

If you have a hard time being honest with your spouse,
you are a candidate for marriage expiration.

If your spouse cannot
even get you to rub or scratch his or her back as a sgn of love and
appreciation, then it might be time for a marital license re-negotiation.

If you do not appreciate
that person who puts up with your crap, your issues, your family, your shortcomings, then
maybe your wedding vows might need rejuvenation.

If you make love to your
mate less than once a week and no other issues prevent intercourse, then you should be
taken outside and given an old-fashioned two-bullet divorce!

If your marriage privileges could be revoked, suspended, or just taken away, that would
prevent most of the stupid crap married people say.

See, the right woman with proper motivation, well she can make a man as hard as a brick,
while the right man with his mind fixed, well he can make a woman do all kinds of sexual
tricks.

So, check yourself and determine how effective you are at being someone's spouse, or you
could be a candidate for marriage expiration and get your butt thrown out of your own
house.

Beauty is a Beast

Whoever told you that beauty
was only skin deep, well, they lied.
See, beauty is not just superficial
true beauty comes from deep inside

your body, or more specifically
it comes straight from the heart.
Stop trying to make people notice you
by over exposing your body parts.

Why do you want a person
to love the false and fake you?
Be real, be honest, be true to yourself,
and please, please get the clue.

Some people get it wrong
or misunderstand things poets say.
Wear your fake hair and stuff if you like,
but don't act like you were born that way.

It's a truly beautiful heart
that a real man seeks.
I have found plenty of beautiful faces
who had the heart of a beast.

If you show me a beautiful woman,
she could be very smart or dumb as a twit,
then I could show you a man
who is sick and tired of her shit.

Some people work all,
day perfecting their superficial look,
when they should be fixing their attitudes,
helping others or learning how to cook.

A beautiful woman and a rich man,
they have the same issue: neither knows if their mate truly loves them or if that love is
superficial.

Do they love your money or facial beauty?
You may never know until it is too late
and you hear that fragile heart
hitting the hard floor.

So, who told you beauty
was actually only skin deep?
Well, it was not a poet!
It must have been a superficial creep.

Some people have lost focus
on what true beauty really is about.
Magazines, videos, media, and those
trying to be in show biz have faked us out.

True beauty is powerful
cannot be contained in a bottle.
I will choose a beautiful heart
over America's next top model.

A dark, bitter, unforgiving heart
can make one ugly from head to toe
but inner beauty shines like a lighthouse
as it causes your heart to glow.

What is true beauty?
I am glad you asked.
Beauty is self-confidence, compassion, intelligence,
love, and understanding, not a make-up mask.

Beauty suffers, beauty works
beauty cares, and beauty prays.
People, when times get tough,
true beauty stays.

Beauty is more than skin deep
open your eyes, come out of the dark.
You can change the outer appearance
but true beauty originates from the heart.

Love Versus Hate

Do I hate to love you, or do I love to hate you?

See, I love how you look at me and how you grow and nurture my seed, but I hate how we argue and yell at one another, although it leads to moments of sure passion under the covers.

I love when we are together; you look at me with those beautiful eyes because I know exactly what you are saying. I hate when we are mad at one another and how you disrespect me in front of my brothers.

I really love how you take care of me, touch and kiss me, while playing your part, because I can tell all that comes directly from your heart.

But I do not understand how you can love me so much right now, and then after one fight, you are ready to throw in the towel.

It is clear you did not pay attention when love was taught in Sunday school.

You also have no concept of how the live by the Golden Rule. I love when you cook for me and make my plate.

It shows me I am your number one, but I hate when you use sex like a gun.

When it comes to you, there is no thin line between love and hate. Right in the middle is where you always seem to operate.

I love when you watch my back and take care of my needs. I hate when you place other things in front of me including my seed.

You are aggressively vindictive, relentlessly angry, and an expert at being rude to others. The problem is, those are your best qualities and that is why it is hard for you to keep a lover.

Yes, I was your man, your number one, because it is your heart I slew. But until you get these things right, leave me alone because you make me hate to love you!

CHAPTER II
Some Kind of Hate

The Warning Shot

I have a master's degree in business and a PhD in life.
Before you mess with me, seek some guidance,

                                        you might need some better advice.

        See you might have a problem with men
        but I am a black educated poet with a pen.

                Do not get it twisted, you need to get it right
                if you jump in my yard, be prepared to fight.

But I am a lover, not a fighter by trade.
I joined the Army on a dare one day.

                I raised my hand and signed on the line.

                Now I write poetry in my spare time.

Who are you?

Baby girl, will the real you stand to your feet?
  Oh no, no, no, please leave all that fake hair in your seat.

      See, I do not even know who you are.
      Girl, you look one way today and you look totally different tomorrow.

Who are you, girl, for heaven's sake?
I cannot even tell because so much of you is fake.

      You have fake hair, a fake nose,
            fake nails, fake eyes, and fake breast, what the hell?

Look at that makeup caked all over your face.
Foundation, eyeliner, and mascara tattooed on, so it cannot be erased.

      We dated for months and I loved those eyes,
            but little did I know, even that was a lie.
You have a fake butt, fake teeth, and Botox lips,
with fake eyelashes and a tummy tuck, are those even your hips?

      You always turn the lights out when I unhook your bra.
      Now I know you were trying to hide those body scars.
Do not talk to me about who's real or who's fake.
When half the stuff on you is synthetic and slipping out of place.

      Who are you baby because I do not even know?
      Girl, you even got your attitude from watching Oprah Winfrey show. You are just
synthetic and so fake, oh my God!
Now tell me, who's the real fraud?

      So, do not get mad, leave, or try and break my heart,
            because I have the receipts right here for half of your body parts!

What have you done for me?

God said, "Let us make man in our image," and then He made you to be man's helpmate.
You were created for a purpose but continue to be corrupted by outside influences!
Get back to what you were created for!

Help me when I struggle. Do not be the reason I am struggling.
Hold me when I do not know I need to be held.
Support me, mentally and physically.
Pray for me if you want me to change.

I have battles all around me, but the last place I want to fight is in my own home.
If fighting is what you are about—criticizing, demeaning, belittling, nagging, degrading,
and being hateful, then get the hell out!

I can say those famous words too and, I can do bad; without having to feed you.
So, leave me if you like, heck you can even change teams by riding a different bike.
I will be ok, no doubt I will recover—as a matter of fact, your best friend wants to be
my new lover.

So

So, you want to be someone's Queen?
Then, get your butt off that video screen!

Yes, I agree, a good man is hard to find,
especially when all you have going on is your big behind!

I will say this once and you can remember it forever,
hell naw you are not light as a feather.

Do not ask if you look fat in those jeans; get it straight, those
jeans are a size five and you know you are a seven or an eight!

Yes, Yes, Yes, a good man is hard to find, especially when
he is hiding from your crazy behind.

So you want someone to treat you right,
try not staying out all freaking night.

I hope you do not think that because you gave him a little ass,
that will keep you from moving from first to last.

You say, "A good black man is hard to find," every single day, but that is just not something I
have ever heard a white woman say!

Here is something else because you may not have heard this,
you are the worst customers and you suck at customer service.

If I have offended you then good,
because it's for your own health.

Stop judging others and fix your own self.

Here is some advice just for you:
  Wear clothes that cover all your assets!

  Speak kindly of others, whether you think they deserve it or not.
       Oh my goodness, here's a mandate: it's not always fashionable to be late.

             Finally, stop looking for "Captain-save-a whole lot of people."

Do it right once and save us all from the sequel.

Snap If You Know This Woman

I love women, I truly do, but who in the world needs 100 pairs of shoes?

Gold digging is your main biz, and paternity tests were created because she does not know who her baby daddy is?

Here is a plan, have another baby and take that father to court because some women live off child support.

I ask the question, I was not trying to be mean,

but half the women surveyed have experimented with the other team!

I am going to call out your girl and I may not be talking about you but snap if you know this to be true!

You know a lady who slept with her best friend's man.

You know a straight lady who has experimented with homosexuality.

You know a woman who left a man for a woman who looks like a man!

You know a lady who has held a grudge so long, she cannot remember why.

You know a lady who only has male friends because she cannot get along with or be trusted by other women.

You know a woman who does not clean house very well.

You know a woman who is afraid a maid might take her man!

You know a lady that needed a paternity test to identify her baby's daddy.

You know a woman who does not understand that when it comes to freshness either you are, or you are not—there is no in between.

You know a lady who thinks the microwave is really cooking.

You know a woman who had another baby for more child support.

You know a lady whose food order is never right when she goes out to eat.

You know a lady who is never wrong, and everything is always someone else's fault.

You know a lady who is in customer service and she has the worst people skills you have ever seen.

Please, do not be this woman!

Tell Them To STOP

MONDAY: Hello Miss, no I do not think we have ever met before, but thanks anyway for the compliment and yes, I have been told that I have pretty eyes. Look, I am sorry, but I don't go home with complete strangers, thanks for the offer, but sorry, I do not know you like that!

TUESDAY: Ma'am, the building you are looking for is right in front of you. Thanks for the compliment, but sorry no, I do not date married women. Oh, so you are not happily married? Well, that's not really my problem. Do you think sleeping around will make your marriage better?

WEDNESDAY: I'm sorry, I cannot take your number. *Why?* Because, girl, you have a man, right? *(Why yes, I do, but what does that have to do with you and me getting together?)* Well, it actually has more to say about you than anything else. If you are not happy with him then fix it or leave him, but don't try and pull others into your mess.

THURSDAY: Hello. Why do you need to know what kind of car I drive? Yes, I do have a job, yes, I do have my own house, and yes, I am educated. Hold on one minute, what would you bring to this relationship? Oh, nothing? Well then, this conversation is about over, but you need to know that I am not raising grown ass women, spoiling them while feeding your crack-like shopping habit for the privilege of having you in my life. Thanks, but hell no!

FRIDAY: Hello Kim, how are you doing? No, your girl and I are not together anymore, but you already knew that. How did you know I had an itch right there? Wait, please do not touch me like that. I cannot get with you. I dated your best friend and you were like a sister. What's wrong with you?

SATURDAY: Hello ma'am how are you doing? Thanks for the compliment, but I am not into older women. But it is good to finally meet a strong woman who knows what she wants and has some goals and direction for her life. But, I have my own car, so I don't need to borrow yours. I have my own place, and I do not feel comfortable moving in with you. Are you trying to buy me? Because I am not for sell. Didn't you and my mother go to high school together?

SATURDAY (part 2): Well hello, how are you? Africa sounds beautiful! So are you there on vacation? Because your web page says that you are from the states. Oh, you are visiting family in Africa, but you have been there for over 6 months. Wow, that's a long visit. Look, I am not in love with you ok? And no, I will not send you $487.93. And hell no, you cannot come and live with me. Good bye!

SUNDAY: Look, why are you trying to hook me up with your girl when you know that she has so many issues? You don't even like being around her yourself, so what do you think I am going to do with her? Please tell her to stop calling me and stop driving by my place. I know it is her who keeps calling and hanging up. Please stop following me and no I am not interested in seeing her again. I am not a doctor, but even I know that she is three steps past crazy. She needs help.
What a week.

Something Just Is Not Right

Baby Girl, you are as beautiful as can be,
but you have the sex appeal of a dead tree.

What is it with your hair?
Get it fixed right now as people are really starting to stare.

Look, as we get older we all might get a little big,
but you cannot keep wearing that same old dirty wig.

About that formal dinner, when you were looking your best,
you need to know you looked ridiculous with those tattoos across your breast.

In public, you are so loud girl, it just is not right!
When you talk it sounds like you are having a fist-fight.

I really do not know what you have against make-up, my sweet,
and would you please do something about your rough and crusty feet.

I do not understand why you always have your chest so bare,
then get mad when men, boys, and women stop to stare.

You might want to update your wardrobe a little bit,
because I am tired of seeing you squeeze into that tight shit.

You are a hater; yes, that is the best way to describe you, I think,
and please stop walking around here like your twat does not stink!

Because it does, and it is hard describing you without being rude,
but you are a gold-digging, two-faced, liar who acts like a dude.

Yes, you act like a dude and our personalities clash.
Do not think everyone has not noticed your beard and mustache!

I can get past all the other stuff, for heaven's sake,
but your nasty attitude and mean spirit are just more than I can take.

You wake with an attitude, as nothing is ever right.
Every day is the same; you are mad and all you want to do is fight.

Sometimes you are sweet and nice, that part is true,
but damn, I should not have to get drunk just to sleep with you.

I just cannot believe all the bullshit you put me through.
Remember, you are alive only because it is illegal to kill you.

Bitter B's

They have perfected the method
of driving people away
and they have got the nerve to say:
"All good men or women are married, locked up, or gay!"

You put others through all types of
drama and expect them to stay.
Oh yes, sign me up for some extra
drama after working all damn day!

Nagging, gripping, fussing, complaining,
and expecting someone to just take it
but give me one good reason
why I should put up with that shit.

There is no sex in this world
good enough for me to stay in this trap,
enduring your bull while
listening to your crap.

You've got me
fighting to get free
I prayed to God that you
would just wake up and leave.

Since when was it my job to get you
over your insecurities and bad dreams,
and then work all night to boost your low self-esteem?

Look at your actions and one day
you will realize you are deranged
dragging your old issues into our relationship
expecting the result to change.

Take everything you came here with
including your bad attitude.
I will pay for you to get the hell out of here
before I become completely unglued.

Two is company, three is a crowd—unless
you are dealing with a bitter "b".
Then you will realize that being alone
is the absolute shit!

Misery does love company so stay off that course.
Damn, I should have given you
a two-bullet divorce.

One more thing before you leave
And how could I forget?

You have to be the center of attention, keep up unnecessary
drama, and I regret letting you trap me with sex!
Now run, call your girlfriends
and tell them that,

You Bitter "B".

Sexual Death

Yes, I have been called a fucking genius
when it comes to using my penis.

I once heard a female poet say this with no regards for his health: She said
"If you're a man and you have a three-inch penis, go outside and kill yourself."

Sounds reasonable if you are shallow and think like this, I guess,
but from a man's point of view, I too, have a few requests.

If a man can put his arm up to the elbow in your vagina, please kill yourself!
Hold on because if you do not give head, go jump off the nearest bridge

and listen up, because this may be a little graphic.
If you use sex as a weapon, then go play in highway traffic.

Male or female, if you are ok with having sex once a week or even less for some,
then please eat a heavy dose, of fast acting, adult strength, rat poison.

If you do not wash daily and your vagina smells like old limburger cheese!
Douche first and then go outside and kill yourself please.

There is nothing a man can do with a funky ass twat. Now you have my car,
house, and my bed smelling sour and you have got my stomach all twisted up in knots.

And lady, during sex, go easy on my fucking balls.
NO DAMN teeth during oral sex at all.

We are having sex or making love, not practicing war.
Pain is bullshit and you've made my whole-body sore.

I promised my mother I would respect women until the day I die,
but if you put your fingers near my ass again, I'll black your fucking eye!

So, if you have a little penis, I really feel sorry for thee,
just master eating pussy and leave the real fucking to a genius like me.

CHAPTER III
Sensually Speaking

SHE

She looks like she is lovable, taste-able, and sex-able.
She looks like she bathes in clouds.
She looks like she is bendable and flexible and like she is safety, home, paradise.

She stands like she is planted or built with perfection; like she is the center of attention. All eyes are on her and - she stands like she cannot be moved.

She walks like she is listening to a smooth groove.
She walks with purpose, like she knows exactly where she is going.
She walks like she has been there before.
She walks with determination, conviction, and confidence.

She smells like candy, love, flowers, and a walking air freshener.
She smells like beautiful if it had a scent. Like she is from heaven sent.
Perfection if I am able to lament. Fresh baked cookies: yes, that is her scent.

She sits like she is floating on air, like she is actually standing.
She sits like royalty.

She sits with dignity and respect and while
she sits, she is still the center of attention.

She speaks like she drips with confidence and intelligence.
She speaks like she is educated, graduated, and she speaks with authority.
She speaks with love, wisdom, vision, and clarity, like an oracle.
She speaks with honesty, integrity, and it is clear she can speak on multiple levels because she speaks all five love languages.

She fucks like her rent is due.
She fucks like tomorrow she has a ten-years prison sentence to do.
She fucks like her life depends on it. Like it is the last dick she will ever get.
She fucks like she invented this dick. Like she knows what lovemaking is all about.
She fucks like a master therapist, healing, soothing, and calming all fears.
She fucks like this is her profession; I am just guessing,
she fucks and leaves no questions.
She fucks like her pussy is medication and like this is what she was put on earth to do. She
fucks like she knows how to make love to you!

The Best Ever

Listen up and close your eyes
no, really close them as you envision this.
Open your mind's eye because I want to take you back
in time, as we reminisce.

Just sit back and relax,
trust me you will be glad,
I want you to think back
to the best sex you ever had.

You remember, right there, that sex
when you really didn't care who hears?
That kind of sex you would have
if you had not had any for years.

The sex that when you think about it
your body tingles and your hair sprouts.
The kind of sex that will make you scream
and then tell you friends all about.

The kind of sex you would have if you knew
you were going to prison for life
or the kind of sex you would have
if you just got out of jail last night.

I hope you have that vision, keep your eyes
closed, because I don't want this to end.
This is the kind of sex that screws

you right, over and over again.

This kind of sex will make
a non-smoker take a drag.
Hell, this sex has turned a lot of
People into moms and dads.

Now that I have taken you
to that very special place,
I want to tell you about two of the sexiest things
ever said during sex, right to my face.

Just so you can understand,
I want to tell you a little about me.
You need to know everything here
is for the "Grown and sexy!"

The first situation begins with me
locked in an oral embrace.
She was working me like her life depended on it,
while she was giving me face.

She polished and stroked me like she was trying
to keep herself from being deported.
She worked me so good I don't even think
she realized I involuntarily farted.

Then I exploded, came down like the world
trade and she took my DNA in a huge bunch.

She leaned back, looked at me, licked her lips and said
"You had pineapples and strawberries for lunch!"
WOW, that was one of the sexiest
things I had ever heard in bed.

Hell, I just realized that a true
professional had just given me head.

The next scenario began as she entered
the room see everything went just right.
We were going at it like heavy weight boxers
in a twelve-round championship fight.

Or professional wrestlers because every move
was countered by an even better position.
So, I just started making up moves
because she put up no resistance.

Her final move was an all-out frontal attack.
She had my legs on her shoulders while I was on my back.

She almost got me but not with
the sex; it was what she said.
She looked me in the eyes and said,
"Baby just relax" which just fucked up my head.

Relax? What? That was a total sexual contradiction for me at that time.
Hell, I was as hard as trigonometry relaxing would have been a war crime.

I could not believe what I heard,
trying to understand what she'd just said
it was such a very sexy thing
to say to your man while in bed.

So, I went with the flow and relaxed
because that is what she requested.
Ohhh shit, it actually worked, she was good,
and clearly, I was being tested.

Here is where college helps you in everyday life.
I had to used physics and leverage to come out on top that night.

I put her on her back, her legs on my shoulders
(pay attention this move is a keeper)
I put my feet on the wall and pushed for leverage
(that will put you in a couple inches deeper)

Hell yes, new pussy, that "G" spot, but hold
those legs because she might start kicking,
but fellas, if you are not long enough, dismount,
get on your knees and just get to licking.

Now, when I count to three, open your eyes slowly but keep listening to me.
We are coming back to reality; here we go one, two, and three.

Tomorrow, when you go about your day or whenever you might feel sad.
I want you to think back, smile, and remember
the best sex you ever had.

Pre-Sex

1. (She) I'm almost ashamed how you had me mesmerized.
   Losing all thought, as I looked into those hazel, bedroom eyes.

2. (She) It seemed like a voodoo spell was placed upon me
   controlling my pussy, making it reach for you and leak.

3. (She) Quivering, shivering—what are you doing to me?
   Desperately wanting all your fucking sexual energy.

4. (He) I was thinking the same thing. You look like my chocolate covered desert.
   Your perfume controls me and I would love to watch you slip out of that skirt.

5. (He) We have chemistry, you are so sexy, and I have to mention, I'm already hard. See,
   you have my dick standing at attention.

6. (She) I have never ever felt quite like this.
   I want to be submerged in your kiss.

7. (He) I drew your warm and ready body close and kissed those luscious lips. I felt a
   welcoming embrace with my hands around those rhythmic hips.

8. (She) Passion and heat filled the room; this was foreplay at its best. Then I looked you in
   your eyes and stroked that delicious chest.

9. (He) Emotionally alive and so ready, I could cut right through the sexual tension. I led her
   to her bedroom with no questions and no apprehensions.

10. (She) Leave the lights on, Baby, and watch your head.
    Take off your clothes and come join me in bed.

11. (He) I got out of my clothes, in one smooth motion, ready to fuck! Reminded me of
    Richard Prior in the movie "Which Way is up?"

12. (He) Butt naked and rock hard, I got in bed for some sexual healing. Then, I noticed mirrors all around the room, even on the damn ceiling.

13. (She) Mr. Speaker, I have been waiting an extremely long time to get my legs wrapped around your arms, back, and behind.

14. (He) Strapped and bounded, I entered her body and it was like a grand homecoming, cheers, applause, a standing ovation. I even thought I heard a choir humming!

15. (She) You just don't know see it is hard to explain,
    but I love it when you hold me and call out my name.

16. (Me) Princess, Princess, here I go deep inside letting you know I want it all. One leg wide to the right while the other leg is penned to the fucking wall.

17. (Her) Our skin melted like heat applied to a chocolate box. When your "Outer" entered my "Inner" smoother than Courvoisier over the rocks.

18. (He) Thirty minutes later, I still had not hit bottom nor reached your sweet spot. So, I flipped that butt over, mounted from the back to give it another shot.

19. (She) I was being used as an instrument: twisting,
    existing, of his coexisting for an edible reminiscing.

20. (He) Now, doggie style is the position and I love this action, standing with my boots on, for better traction.

21. (She) Maneuvered like a sexual engineer, (or better, like a cervical domineer), that clouds my celestial sphere and we've only hit second gear.

22. (He) Thirty minutes and five songs later, she showed no signs of slowing down. So, I placed her on top and then she really began to pound.

23. (She) I liked this position best because I'm in control, and that's no mystery. It felt so good I was shaking like I got hit by a bolt of electricity.

24. (He) I lost track of time, but three orgasms later, she slid to one side. So, I put her legs on my shoulders, my feet on the wall, and went even deeper inside.

25. (She) It was like fucking a fantasy of consummation while tearing sheets, eating pillows, and suffering from serious dehydration.

26. (He) On top again, I felt my body responding to all this hustle and bustle. While making love to you, I think I used every one of my damn muscles.

27. (She) I couldn't control it, couldn't hold it, was about to give in with no fear. These mirrors were watching me release more of my sticky souvenirs.

28. (He) I hope I'm not hurting you, because that is the wrong message, but sometimes, when I'm in the act, I get completely aggressive.

29. (She) My legs were so wide, I think you touched my kidney, hell, from my bladder to my intestines, I am completely empty.

30. (He) One more orgasm from this position, as I gripped her butt. Finally, I came, body tight, toes curled, heavy breathing, feeling great, totally relaxed, and eyes shut.

Bed Hustler

I am your bed hustler and I am your cat rustler.
I am your sexual instructor and I am your vagina conductor.

I can make your vajayjay communicate properly,
Jumping, leaking, sweating—all involuntarily.

Orchestrating your multiple orgasms,
while filling your body with passion.

Making you pop on demand.
Got it responding to all my commands.

I will pluck you good that's right,
and afterwards you will not care about my height.

Because I am your vaginal controller,
filling your room with after-sex smells.

Big-fanny women get this work while
looking at your toenails.

You want to be the best tango of my life?
Get your butt back over here and make me cum twice.

Hell, three times if you have time!
I really like smashing after the orgasm if you do not mind.

Baby girl, I will beat your weave sideways,
and that's no lie.

Give me the chance and I will pound you
until you are paralyzed,

temporarily, because this experience, well is a team sport,
match, or game.

I want to give it to you so good, you will get a
tattoo with my name,

because I am your butty-bouncer
and your breast-stroker.

I'm your midnight vulva stimulator and
your PP, (that's Poonany Poker).

Yes, I'm your clitoris collaborator
and I am your headache stopper.

I know you may have a migraine and
feel under the weather,

so I covered my manhood with aspirin, and
if you suck it, we will both feel a lot better.

After Sex

1. (Him) Deep sniff, Bernie Mac coined the term "BADUSSY,"
   which is the combination of butt, dick, and pussy!

2. (Him) Tell me, it was just the two of us in here right,
   because there was so much action in here last night.

3. (Him) Your tongue, wow, you have skills, no doubt.
   Ok, now I need to know: Was that ice in your mouth?

4. (Him) Please, please, please, don't fucking touch my nipples right now.
   Well, that is unless you're ready to go one more round.

5. (Him) Damn, the sun is coming up and I've got to go make my ends.
   But, could you please do that thing with your tongue, once again?

6. (Her) Your arms wrapped around my waist; I love the smile I put on your face.

7. (Her) But Baby, I was thinking, don't be greedy. Share your body; give me a taste.

8. (Him) Wow, that was spectacular! You have remarkable skill! That thing you
   did with the hot water in your mouth gave me such a fucking thrill.

9. (Her) You had me open in layers from our sexual rotator.
   How in the world did you know blueberries are my favorite fruit flavor?

10. (Him) Baby, your oral skills are great, you made me so ready.
    I'm glad you were naked, although I could have fucked you right through your teddy.

11. (Her) I can feel your touch and even taste you when I close my eyes.
    I am exhausted; hell, I cannot feel anything between my thighs.

12. (Him) You're so flexible and your balance is unbelievable! You have so many tricks!
    Where in the hell did you learn that shit, and what did you do to my dick?

13. (Her) Baby, all these countless hours you made me reach my plateau, especially head first, I found my very own Jacques Cousteau.

14. (Him) Goose bumps, toes curling, and body releasing, so have no concern. Heavy breathing, body empty, I'm laying here making more sperm.

15. (Her) You are my pussy masseuse and I am glad you are mine. I love when you take control of my entire body, including my insides.

16. (Him) Never wanted or even thought this is something I would say: but you've got me volunteering to be your fucking sex slave.

17. (Her) The dream, now a reality, so the desire cannot be controlled since I was pulled by a force, then ignited to explode.

18. (Him) My favorite moves happened while you rode me, (I hope you did not mind). I pressed your breast together and suck both your nipples at the same time.

19. (Her) I loved it when you went deeper, like searching for King Tut. When you flipped me over, head down and up in the air was my butt.

20. (Him) I've really got to go to work, but I want to stay: hell, I am so perplexed. Damn Baby, I fucking love the smell of our after-sex.

Sex Education

Plucking should be my legal profession because I am always giving lessons during these sex sessions.

My goal is to give you a permanent happy facial expression
and clear you of any clinical depression.

So, take my love making course, please
and you can earn your copulation degree.

Minor in oral sex and get some extra credit if you master ice stimulation.
Upon your graduation, you will have a sexual revelation.

Look, I will teach you how to go "balls deep," but first into their mind.
You will learn to go so deep in a vagina, it will feel like you're committing a crime.

This course teaches you how to curl toes, harden nipples, or get panties wet.
You will master total sexual satisfaction and, better sex, you will get.

Here is a free sexual tip from Mr. Speaker. Listen so you know what to do.
Ladies, if you master this technique, he will never, ever forget you.

Give him oral sex with half of your mouth filled with hot water and him, on a towel and flat on his back.

After a few minutes of stimulation, let the water run right down his crack.

It will feel like a massive orgasm just ran down his seat.
Stop, dry him off, refill your mouth, and repeat.

Fellas, here is an experiment that is really nice;
Time how long it takes her sugar walls to melt a cube of ice.

Melt two or three more cubes of ice, and then dive right in.
It is like making love to hot ice cream, and to your Johnson, this is an amazing sensation.

Men concentrate, do not focus on that chatter,
I don't care what you have heard; size really does matter.

Lastly, here is a fact you can put to the test.
An orgasm can relieve migraines and they can reduce overall stress!

Verbal Lap Dance

Sit down baby, because this could take some time.
> Please place your hands in your lap, as I play with your mind.

Soft lights reflecting, while faint music plays, but the beat comes through clear.
> You're unwinding while I'm grinding, body responding as I draw near.

Now I am standing behind you but we both still have on all our clothes.
> Eyes lids joined as this experience is enhanced by fragrances entering your nose.

Breathe in my aroma, taste me with your imagination.
> Mmmmm, that's right, now lick those lips as you hunger for my sexual and Verbal Vibration.

Now watch as I peel clothes off, like a piece of fruit, allowing my body to breathe.
> I have been held captive by this material, it just won't let my manhood hang free.

Relaxing music, dim lights, candles burning at a distance,
> sit still, hands down as you feast your eyes on my uncovered existence.

Behind you, I stroke your shoulders to the elbows, then your earlobes get a nibble.
> I move slowly so you can catch every ripple, as I gently graze your hard nipples.

Excited by our static connectivity, I move slowly to your thighs.
> Gentle strokes, as you lean your head back and once again close your eyes.

I placed your left foot on my chest, while I massage you from knee to heel.
> My tongue and fingers tickling your toes, now you know how a queen should feel.

I caress each of your legs individually, because they are precious gifts.
> I place my hand in the small of your back and notice your hips start to lift,

but please, remain seated as this dance gets a little heated.
> This is what you have needed. Like a precious gem, is how you are being treated.

I draw close to your moist lips, straddle your body, and unhook your bra strap.
My full weight supported by your thighs, my erect manhood resting on your lap.

Body contact, as we anticipate a passionate kiss, and we both start to lean in.
Eyes closed, I'm hard, you're wet, the music stops, and this dance comes to an end.

New Foreplay

Foreplay does work for many to start the night,
and for me, sex should involve all five senses, if you
want to do it right.

Good sex should involve the entire body, listen to what I say.
We will hit all *five senses,* forget just having regular *four* play.

Touching hands, shoulders, knees, thighs, elbows, and toes,
while making physical contact with every inch of your body. Yes, that's how it goes.

I want to stimulate your sense of sight, smell, hearing, feeling, and taste.
See Baby, real sex, complete sex, includes them all, and is delivered at a slow pace.

First, you have got to be looking good because sex starts with the eyes
and all I want to smell are berries and juices when I open your thighs.

I will grip your hips, so you won't slip, as I dive in face-first, below your waist.
All I want to hear are sex sounds, as I get a good wet and nasty taste.

See, hearing and feeling you react to my actions makes me have muscle contractions.

That's right, I grow thicker as I lick her, but no, I am not ready to stick it there, wait.

Now do me, see, baby taste me, in your mouth, baste me, as you lay waste to me.

It is time for five play to end and for me to go in, damn, I like how you fuckin' bend!
Missionary, scissors, flat on your stomach, doggie style, and then while standing, upside
down, with my feet on the wall, suck my nipples and feel my dick keep expanding.

Now, I am kidney deep, cramp in my leg, don't stop. Is she speaking in tongues?
So damn deep, my dick can feel the air in her lungs.

Hands on my back *touch*, sex in the air *smells* just right,
I can see your legs in the mirror all up in the air through the dim light *sight*.
I *hear* you in concert with the squeaking bed, which ignites my desire. You *taste* my nipples,
causing me to spray navy men all over you, like you are on fire.
My toes curled so tight, they could catch a baseball without a glove.
See Baby, by using our five senses, out of thin air, we just created pure love.

Poetry Prostitution

Poetry for pussy or is it pussy for poetry? Either way,
I am trying to enter you from different places, so come
on and just flow with me today.

Yes, I will pimp my poetry for pussy, and I will use sweet spoken word to get to your gushie gushie.

I will perform poetry for punany.
I will lay hands and dick on your fanny.

Yes, yes, yes; I confess,
I will spit poetry in order to see your breast,
I mean tenderness, and I will sling even more poetry to get you to completely undress.

Poetry for oral stimulation,
more spoken word equals deeper penetration.

Have you ever been talked right out of your
damn drawers?
I am a master negotiator, going deep
until you have verbal withdrawals.

Come on, play strip poetry with me.
Lose on purpose and show me your ass for poetry.

Poetry for pussy; don't forget what I just told ya,
because Mr. Speaker is your true pussy-fucking Soldier.

You   I want to haiku you

I want to immortalize you
in ink, on sheets, between lines, from the front and from behind it is true.
I want to **float** with you

I want to ride slowly with you
I want to get **inside** of you,
and yes Baby, I want to go and come with you
I want to spend hours pleasuring you
I want to discover hidden erogenous zones on you
I want to learn from you
then I want to **teach** you
a thing or two.   I want to feed off you
and if you allow **me**, I will also eat off you

See baby, I am a sexual carnivore because I love this shit.
I eat the pussy first, and then I kill it.
Over and over so keep the music on rewind,
until we both lose our sexual minds.
We will only stop and reflect on the things we do
and plan our next sexual interlude, where we will
attempt **to** reach physical limits before we conclude.

By no means am I through with you
All day **long** I am planning ways to get at you
All I do is think of you Baby, you
inspire me to be better, this is so true.
My body is here, but my mind is in a faraway kind of mood.

I am n **paradise** when I am with you
I cannot even write without thinking of you
Your body has seventeen perfect curves, because you

are my sexual haiku.

Sexy Woman

There is just a certain way a woman with good vajayjay walks.

She moves with confidence because she has his manhood on lock-down, and he is not going anywhere.

See, she makes love like her vagina can actually change lives.

She is constantly over watched by others but; she is never under-sexed by her lover.

She is a pleasant surprise when she crosses your path, and she will put you to sleep if she gives you some ass.

   I want to chase her thoughts as I stalk her beautiful mind.
   I want to spank her words because she is so darn fine.
   I want to tap that ass every time she spits a rhyme.

She is so sexually talented, and she has mastered the mic,
   I want to cover her with so much of my DNA that people say, "You two look alike."

All of this just because of the way she moves and the way she glides.

See, this woman turns beauty into sexy with every stride.

CHAPTER IV
Women I Have Loved

Unseen Romance (A Note about online dating)

Although we have not physically seen each other yet,
  Our conversations are real and deeper than those of lovers.

I feel like our hearts have already met.
  And even though we are still getting to know each other,

I take this step towards you with hope and faith.
  Your voice makes me smile, I even want to dance.

Once our eyes do meet, no more time will we waste.
  You've done all this without even one glance.

I know that all good things must come to an end,
  But we will know God has truly brought us together,

If finding true happiness is when life really begins,
  And this becomes the start of something that could last forever.

My dear, I don't want you to think this a dream.
  I see your beautiful heart and you heal my scars.

You've slain a giant you've never seen.
  I feel drawn to you, from a distance, quite far

So, let's take this step, just give me a chance,
  because this could be the start of your last romance!

Second

She said to me, I am an excellent number two!
What she did not realize was how she just blew

my mind, because her words gave me a jumpstart.
So, I gave her one of my ribs to better protect her heart.

She knows she is designed to watch my back, front, and side.
On top of that, she knows she is my ride or die!

Now she is free to love me. Now she is able to birth my seed.
She is determined to help me succeed. Assisting me is her creed.

She does not fight me for the lead.
I give her more because she has no greed.

She satisfies all my needs and keeps me from misdeeds.
I am so high on her, I could get a nose bleed.

She is my stimulating conversation.
My lady with no complications

She is my peace and stability, so I won't roam.
She makes me want to come home.

Now I know she has my back through and through,
because in a one-on-one relationship,
she's my perfect number two!

My Queen

When you look at me,
my heart skips a beat. I feel I can do anything. I am filled
with courage. My heart becomes strong, and I am filled with confidence.

When you believe in me,
I believe in me. I feel like I can accomplish
anything. There is nothing I cannot do or be.

When you love me,
I have everything I need to accomplish any task. I am taller than any building, stronger than
anything, and ready to protect you at any cost.

When you trust me,
I have confidence. When you care about me, I feel loved
and cherished. When you stand with me, I feel invincible.

When you pray for me,
I am finally equipped properly to do all things, because, to begin to love you, is to never
stop. You are those things that I am not. You came from my rib and now you walk and birth
my seed.

You strong, black woman, the perfect check, and the perfect mate, because mixed with any
other race, you still dominate. You have built nations and birthed kings.
You have loved and educated thousands,
and you were created to be my queen!

Hello Again

Young men desperately need wisdom, while older men long for youth.
The day our eyes met, I knew this was the God's honest truth.

But when our eyes met as we passed through that door,
my heart knew ahead of my brain, that our eyes had met before.

I thought all hope was lost and there was little good left out there for me,
then here you come into my life like a cool, light, autumn breeze.

Just when I was convinced I was on the wrong path, going down the wrong aisle,
here you come with your happy disposition; infectious, beautiful, and intoxicating smile.

Just when I was sure superwoman didn't exist and she was a figment of my imagination,
here you come with your warm embrace, your spiritual, and college education.

See, I normally don't do this or that, but with you, I seem to be taking all that back.

You are the exception to most of my rules.

When I look at your pictures, I actually drool.
I am not the same person you once knew.
My heart has been battered until it is black and blue.

I've been through relationship hell, what a mess.
I made horrible decisions and my heart just needs a rest!

I had all these visions coupled with my huge dreams,
but I had no idea there were so many gold-diggers out to pick my pockets clean.

I am older, wiser and way more cautious while I am out on the town, but I am still looking
for a real queen to share my crown!

A Note to the "I"

I want to love you; I want to have you.
I want to hold you; I want to be inside you.

Inside your thoughts, whether they are happy or blue,
and by your side, making your dreams come true.

You inspire me, and your words move me.
You have touched my heart effortlessly,
and your kindness helps me see.

Your beauty is way more than skin deep;
your beauty starts from inside, then
goes from your head to your feet.

Let my words caress you, as I get next to you.
See, I am trying to express to you,
that I want to always be there to protect you.

You already have my rib; it was given to you at birth.
I've come for your heart because you are my angel or earth.
You are my wise counsel and you are my biggest fan!
You're my biggest cheerleader
that's why I will always be your man.

These phrases were put together with care, this is true.
So, to my beautiful "I," would you please let me love you?

Team Sears

Mine eyes have awakened from an amazing dream,
where I witness the formation of a remarkable team.

We know there is no "I" in team no matter how you spell it.
Except at the heart of Team Sears, the "I" is a perfect fit.

The "I" comes in peace and never causes harm.
She is calm, check out that "I" in the center of the storm.

Heads up and eyes right when she passes by.
She is my queen, so mess with her and I will black both your eyes.

So, my heart and my love to the "I", I commit,
and at the end of every vote, you will hear: "The I's have it."

That means she is always on the winning side,
and to my friend request, yes, is what she replied.

Yes, the "I" is the best, and to mix with her is stupendous.

Together, we form an unbeatable team.
Made up of the "I" and the man of her dreams.

That is my wish, so please be my girl.
One love, that's right, Team Sears to the world.

The "I" Has It

I want more of you, or as much of you as I can get.
Come into my life. I want to explore your heart.
You are my yin, I'm your yang; we are the perfect fit.

I want to study your thoughts like a work of art.
begin with a smile, grows with a kiss, and ends with a tear,
Because that is the day I don't want to comprehend.

but I don't want to see that tear for one thousand years.
See, that point in time is when our love will end.
I want countless intimate conversations with you.

I want to be in your thoughts by day, your dreams at night,
I want even more non-verbal communications (it's true).
and if something is wrong, look to me to make it right.

I want to be your fantasy, your protector, your charmer.
I want to watch you age gracefully,
Baby, I am your knight in shining armor.

and I want to witness God blessing you, continuously.
You are my muse; you are my motivation
You are my help, you give me strength, and you give me peace.

Your voice is my music; your smile is my inspiration
Come share my life, watch our love, and blessing increase.
You are my song and you are my ink,

let these words caress, as I get next to you.
You are my flower; you've changed how I think.
It is my job to protect, and never neglect you.

While lost in the wilderness 40 years, wandering al over the world.
God was perfecting and training me to recognize you; my perfect girl.

Apple Pie

Her smile makes angels blush.
God made her with a special paintbrush.

Classy, sophisticated, with hypnotic eyes,
her complexion makes me think of apple pie.

Warm delicious and perfect at any time of the day,
Her lips are like a soundtrack you would hear on Broadway.

She is striking and stunning,
whether she is walking or running.

Her heart is put together with the finest construction.
I am sure by now you would like an introduction.

Her first name is "Just,"
Her middle name is "So."
Her last name is, "Beautiful!"

Vessel

She is remarkable, she is undisputable,
and she is so unmistakable.

This vessel is old school but with a modern twist, nothing artificial.
Her beauty runs deep see, it's not superficial.

She is light on her feet, adventurous, and so versatile.
Spontaneous, energetic, have you seen this vessel smile?

She is a builder, dancer, and a sweet skater;
She is a filmmaker and a risk taker.

She could be the yang to any yin.
See, with or without makeup, this vessel is always a ten.

Her heart is so bright it could blow your mind.
She even makes her son shine.

I mean she is special no matter the role she is in or the quest.
Check II Corinthians 4 verse 7 as God describes this vessel best.

She looks good in all colors, but this vessel makes red come alive.
The perfect teammate plays any role because she will ride or die.

I want to chase her thoughts and cheer this vessel up when she is blue.
For the rest of my life, I want to be her knight and make all dreams come true.

If you see her it is clear she is headed to a higher level.
That is why in my dreams she is the perfect vessel.

Early Morning Come Back
(After "A Piece of Early Morning Love by Charlzetta Driver)

Now listen! By 6am, I am ready to hit that mark again;
I get aroused when I hear the words "Poet Go In!"

I do, but only for you,
because this poetry session is just for two.

I want to chase your words and stalk your beautiful mind.
I want to spank your thoughts because your poetry is frog's hair fine.

I want to tap your assets every time you spit those lines.
Your melodious words cause me to bust into poetic rhymes.

You are gifted and talented and at 4am you mastered the mic.
I want to cover you with some much of my ink, people say, "You two look alike."

I will defeat writer's block to get to your spit. See, as a military poet, Baby Girl, I am trained and built for this shit.

Just for the record, everything you did two hours ago was foreplay.
You should already know, Soldiers do more by 6am than most poets do all day.
So, next time you slice me a piece of early morning love, make sure it's the weekend or we both will be calling in late to work once again.

CHAPTER V
Biblical Love

Biblical Love Poem

Female:

> Let him kiss me with the kisses of his mouth
> For your love is more delightful than wine
> Pleasing is the fragrance of your perfumes
> Your name is like perfume poured out.
> No wonder the maidens love you.
> Take me away with you, let us hurry!
> Let the king bring me into his chambers

Friends:

> We rejoice and delight in you
> We will praise your love more than wine

Female:

> How right they are to adore you!
> Dark am I, yet lovely, oh daughters of Jerusalem
> Dark like the tents of Kedar, like the tent curtains of Solomon
> Do not stare at me because I am dark,
> because I am darkened by the sun.
>
> My mother's sons were angry with me;
> made me take care of the vineyards;
> my own vineyard I have neglected.
>
> Tell me, you whom I love, where you graze your flock
> and where you rest your sheep at midday.
> Why should I be like a veiled woman beside the flocks
> of your friends?

Male:

> I liken you, my darling, to a mare harnessed to the chariots of Pharaoh.
> Your cheeks are beautiful with earrings, your neck with strings of
> jewels. We will make you earrings of gold, studded with silver.

Female:

> While the king was at his table, my perfume spread its fragrance.
> My lover is to me a sachet of myrrh resting between my breasts.
> My lover is to me a cluster of henna blossom from the vineyards of En Gedi

Male:

  How beautiful you are my darling, Oh how beautiful!
  Your eyes are doves.

Female:

  How handsome you are, my lover! Oh, how charming!
  And our bed is verdant.

Male:

  The beams of our house are cedars; our rafters are firs.

II

She: I am a rose of Sharon, a lily of the valleys.

He: Like a lily among thorns is my darling among the maidens.

She: Like an apple tree among the trees of the forest is my beloved among the young men.
I delight to sit in his shade, and his fruit is sweet to my taste. Let him lead me to the banquet
hall and let his banner over me be love. His left hand is under my head, and his right hand
embraces me. Daughters of Jerusalem, I charge you, by the gazelles and by the doe of the
field: Do not arouse or awaken love until it so desires.

III

The voice of my beloved! Behold, he cometh leaping upon the mountains, skipping upon
the hills. My beloved is like a roe or a young hart: behold, he standeth behind our wall, he
looketh forth at the windows, shewing himself through the lattice. My beloved spake, and
said unto me, "Rise up, my love, my fair one, and come away. For, lo, the winter is past, the
rain is over and gone; the flowers appear on the earth; the time of the singing of birds is
come, and the voice of the turtle is heard in our land; the fig tree putteth forth her green
figs, and the vines with the tender grape give a good smell. Arise, my love, my fair one, and
come away.

IV

These paraphrased words
that were spoken were not from my hand.

See, these words
were inspired by God and
written by King Solomon!

These few words were
taken from the Bible,
this you can believe.

Just open up the word
and count 22 books in
and there you will see.

They are right there
in the open with no
guessing or mystery,

and what you will find
is one of the oldest
love poems in history.

*Words from Songs of Solomon

Love Story

Love makes the world go 'round so I invite you to listen to this with your heart. Today, I will tell you one of the greatest love stories I have ever found.

King Solomon was a brave, strong, wealthy and powerful king during his time, and according to the Bible, he was the wisest man to ever walk the earth. Queen Makeda was, the beautiful, virgin Queen of Sheba, Nubia, Kush, and Axum, modern day Ethiopia. About 1000 years before Christ, King Solomon decided to build a magnificent temple to honor YAHWEH and sent messengers to invite all countries to Jerusalem to see the temple and trade. During that time, Ethiopia was second only to Egypt in power and fame, and was well-known for beautiful people, rich history, deep spiritual traditions, and wealth. An Ethiopian merchant named Tamrin took stories of King Solomon's wealth compassion and wisdom to Queen Makeda, inspiring her to visit Jerusalem.

The Queen's visit was extraordinary. She came with a massive train of camels bearing spices, lots of gold and other precious stones greater than any gifts King Solomon ever received, about $3.6 million in today's terms. Just imagine the sight of 797 camels, donkeys and mules too numerous to count, crossing the Sahara Desert, led by a beautiful black Queen. King Solomon already had 700 wives and concubines. He had enough women in his life and did not need any more. Yet, King Solomon was so enthralled by her beauty, he did all he could to accommodate Queen Makeda. He had an apartment built, gave her the best foods, and 11 changes of garments daily.

King Solomon responded to her thirst for knowledge by having a throne set up for the Queen right next to his, so she could listen as he delivered judgments. The Queen traveled and observed the King as he interacted with his subjects in everyday affairs. The Queen said, *"How happy I am when I interrogate you! How happy when you answer me! My whole being is moved with pleasure; my soul is filled; my feet no longer stumble; I see light in the darkness; I am thrilled with delight; how happy I am; I would remain here always, if but as the humblest of your workers so that I could always hear your words and obey you."*

King Solomon was completely enamored by the young Ethiopian Queen and wrote about her in the Songs of Solomon. The King held elaborate banquets in her honor, and entertained her during her stay, but they both knew she must remain a virgin.

But the King had fallen in love with the young Queen and tried to figure out a way around ancient Ethiopian tradition. After six months in Israel, Queen Makeda announced *"I must return home,"* so the King invited her to a magnificent farewell dinner. The meal lasted for several hours and featured hot and spicy foods, by order of the King. Since the meal ended very late, the King invited the Queen to remain overnight in his quarters. She agreed, as long as the King would not take advantage of her.

The King agreed to honor her chastity as long as she honored his request that she not take anything in the palace. Outraged by the suggestion that she was a thief, the Queen promised not to take anything from the palace. Later that evening and dying of thirst, the Queen drank water she found in the palace. The King came up and stated she broke her oath and had taken from the palace. The Queen protested that the oath should not cover

something as insignificant and plentiful as water. The King told her there was nothing in the world more valuable than water, for without it nothing would live. Released from his oath, the King took the Queen as his 701st lover. The King placed a ring on her hand and stated, "If you have a son, give him this ring and return him to me."

The Queen had a son and called him *"Son of the Wise Man,"* heir to the throne. The young King's name was Menelik, meaning *"How Handsome He Is."* Solomon's first-born son visited his father and was anointed King of Ethiopia, transferring monarchy from matriarchy to a patriarchy at the Queen's request. When Menelik returned to Ethiopia, the King sent all the first-born sons of his leaders to Ethiopia with him and it is believed the Ark of the Covenant went also.

This famous line has continued down to the 20th century when, even now, the ruler of Ethiopia is the "Conquering Lion of Judah," descended directly from King Solomon and Queen Makeda.

A Good Thing

Who can find a virtuous woman? I am just asking.

Who can find a woman so precious she is worth more than fine jewelry and her husband's heart finds complete safety while in her possession?

Who can find a woman strong enough to do good to her husband and not evil even when she might feel completely justified because he has done wrong?

Who can find a woman that can balance motherhood
and a career with being a wife? Who can find her?

She hugs with compassion, counsels with wisdom, scolds with understanding, cooks with love, and disciplines with a firm hand. I ask you, where is she?

She is selfless, giving, loving, honest, peaceful, protective, intelligent, wise, diligent, hardworking, kind, generous, caring, and sexy. *Who* can find her?

She is up early, providing for her household and she stays up late, making sure all is in order. See, she does what needs to be done to make a house a home.

Her husband has confidence in her, in her decisions, and in her abilities. He loves her because she always does him good.
I am looking for her.

She is intelligent, she plans, she coordinates, she manages, she educates, and she trains. She is dependable and reliable because her word is honest and true.

She does what she says she will do. She walks her talk and not by gossiping to others. Whether wealthy or poor, college educated or not, she is a queen!

Day or night, at home or in the streets, she honors herself and her home. She is more than bilingual, she speaks all five love languages, and whatever she puts her hands to is good!

Good like ice-cold water when you thirst or like actors need to rehearse.

She is good like sick people need a nurse or like songs need a verse.
She is good like directions when you are lost or like a big mac with that special sauce.
She is good like a phone call when you need a friend or finding $20 when you need ten.
She is good like giving sight to the blind, like freedom to the confined, or like she is a good thing a man has been blessed to find.

She is so good because out of her mouth comes wisdom and no lies.
She knows in God is where her strength resides.

Her family calls her blessed, for her husband she provides complete rest, and he always listen to her because he knows she is his good thing. There is no way to measure her worth. She is more valuable than anything as love was put into her at birth.

Tell me, *who* can find a virtuous woman?

Forgive

Forget with no regret and forgive so you can live,
that is my message I stepped up here to give.

Forgiving is process, a necessity, and an obstacle you must pass. Someone has had to forgive you before, just look into your past.
People who hold grudges are really only holding themselves down, while the individual they will not forgive, has moved on to higher ground.

The moment you forgive, you release all the things holding you in place. You release pain, misery, strife, suffering, and all kinds of other things, into space.

Forgiveness is powerful. It is rejuvenating, strength, and life. Good things come to the person who forgives; and that is nice.
One of the last things said while being crucified was a prayer with a request. Not a prayer for self, but a prayer for God to forgive, because "they know not what they do," He stressed.
The Savior used his last words to pray God forgive those who beat him and took his life. Even while His flesh was dying, He was showing us what was right.

So please forgive anyone you feel like has wronged or hurt you. Once you forgive them, many more blessing will come, now that is true.

CHAPTER VI
Love Wins

Love or Hate?

Love verses Hate is the classic battle of good versus evil.
Stand clear because this battle has been very lethal,
taking lives, breaking hearts and leaving grave yards filled,
because everyone in this fight gets killed.
Spread love not hate, or you will see,
years of misery will come to thee.
Even if a person is out to cause you harm,
return their efforts with love but keep them at arms
Distance because they still cannot be trusted.
while trust is earned so don't get them twisted

Love is given	
Love gives while	hate takes.
Love binds while	hate breaks.
Love is gentle, and	hate is not.
Love is kind and	hate has bad thoughts.
Love is free, but	hate could cost you your crown.
Love is happy while	hate slowly breaks you down.

See, hate controls you and never heals.
Hate hardens hearts and your spirit it kills.
Many times, the enemy just wants a little
hate to enter your heart.
That is when your troubles actually start.
Keep your head, protect yourself, and fight off
hate with no remorse.
I learned this valuable lesson during my divorce.
Refuse bitterness no matter how bad things escalate.
Love is always a better option than hate.

Rumble! (Trust vs. Love)

Ladies and Gentlemen,

    In the red corner we have the challenger from parts unknown, the number one contender and one of the necessary things you need for a happy home.

This contender is critical and for complete happiness, it is a must. Please put your hands together and let me hear it for the undefeated challenger, TRUST.

And in the opposing corner, we have the reigning leader from high above, the undisputed, undefeated, untied, champion of the world, LOVE.

This is a historic bout as either of these competitors could make a relationship stumble. Ladies and Gentlemen, hold on to your seats and LET'S GET READY TO RUMBLE!

TRUST comes out swinging with
lefts of loyalty and rights of righteousness.
LOVE was on the defensive blocking blows
while everyone was watching this.

TRUST pressed the attack with hits of honor
followed by right of respect,
while LOVE bobbed and weaved
using compassion as a shield to deflect.

Exhausted, TRUST looked at LOVE
and threw a devastating blow.
TRUST said, "There is no possible way you can have
a loving relationship without me you know."

LOVE hit TRUST with the Bible repeatedly
and this is what was heard:
"LOVE thy neighbor as thyself,"
now that is written word.

LOVE endures long,
LOVE is patient, and love is kind.
LOVE does not envy, is not jealous,
does not boast, so get in line.

LOVE bears, **BELIEVES**, hopes, and endures all things, which is a must.
LOVE is not conceited, it is not rude, and never **fails** unlike TRUST.
Dazed and confused, by
these biblical combinations, TRUST fell apart.
LOVE then said: "TRUST in the **Lord** with all thy heart."

God is LOVE, so TRUST in Him and you will never fall.
And still the undefeated champion of the world, because
LOVE conquers all!

Love Talk

Do you know your love language? I mean, do you even know how to communicate your love to the one you love?

Author Gary D. Chapman taught us how to communicate love in his book titled "The Five Love Languages." For those who have not read this book, here is your lesson.

Nothing is really free; it will cost time and you need to pay attention. There are five love languages or ways to communicate love.

The Five Love Languages are:

Words of affirmation, quality time, physical touch, gifts, and my personal favorite, acts of service which is my love language just in case someone out there wants to show me some love.

Words of Affirmation – compliments, encouraging, positive, constructive words - just saying "You are beautiful" or "I love you."

Quality Time – date night; eating meals together; face-to-face or over the phone; taking walks; doing things together one-on-one, mostly but not exclusively.

Physical touch is just what is says – holding hands, hugs, spooning or just sitting close, yes this does include sex or love making for you educated types.

Gifts really needs no detailed explanation, but the gifts actually need to be something your loved one desires, do not give chocolates to a flower person.

Acts of Service – Helping your mate, taking care of your mate or their needs; watching their back see, for me this is the best way to communicate love.

Now that you know what the five love languages are, you must determine which one is the most important one to you.

The next step is very important; find out your partner's love language.

Some people get these love languages confused because they believe physical touch may be everyone's number one language.

If you call some people hateful or derogatory names all day, it is possible they might not have a desire to love on you later that night, just because you are now in the mood.

Or two extremely busy individuals might realize that quality time is the main thing lacking in their lives due to their busy schedules.

Additionally, do not get a gift confused with quality time. They might just want you there, whether you have a gift or not. Sometimes, showing up is the gift.

Acts of Service ranks high with me because this love language gets at the heart of God's design and overall purpose for the woman, which is to be a helpmate.

If you are not helping him or her in some way, shape, form, or fashion, then you may just be a burden to them.

So, determine your love language. It helps you communicate so much better, because many are talking and no one understands what we are saying.

Remember, your love life is a reflection of your ability to communicate.

The Language of Respect

Do you speak his language of respect? You may not, even if you two speak the same dialect.

Allow me to break this down; there are a few things to correct,
There indeed, is such a thing as the language of respect.

This could be the reason why men and women do not always understand each other.
Women speak the language of love while men learned respect from their father or mother.
Trust me, this topic is deep so here is an example from a king;
Have you ever observed three women talking?
They talk over each other and cut each other off with no objections. For some women, this is considered a normal conversation.
If you ladies try to speak with a man this way, you could see your man with another woman that very day.

Men generally view this type of conversation as disrespectful, rude, and very frustrating.

Speaking to a man as if he is a woman could be devastating, to your relationship and your ability to get your point across and to be understood.

Here are some ways to show respect to the man you love and how you can make him feel good:

Let him finish his sentences even if you know what he is going to say,
  Offer, do not force assistance

Be on time! Do what you say you are going to do.
  Give him his love language.
  Look him in his eyes.
  Fight fair; leave the past in the past.
  Pick your battles, if everything is a fight, he could just withdraw.
  Respect him by respecting yourself.
  Do not put your business in the street to people who talk too much.
  Be sincere and show gratitude (and less, attitude)

Compliment his achievements.
Learn to respectfully disagree but support anyway if he has the lead.
Honor his opinions, abilities, and follow the house rules.

One more thing before I end this manuscript: men tend to disrespect their own, while women tend to disrespect other people's relationships.

Keep your head up, hang in there, do not get shook.
More information on this topic is coming soon in my new E-Book.

Battle Buddy

Issued to you when you join the military for your protection.
  Your battle buddy goes with you no matter the direction.

  Let me break this down so you battle-understand.
Your battle buddy is your first military friend.

Your battle buddy is like family but much tighter.
  If you need words, then your buddy is the battle-writer.

  Your keeper of record if that is what you battle-need.
Your battle buddy always follows your battle-lead.

Unless you battle-follow them on the next mission!
  Battle buddies are truly an Army tradition.

  You do everything with your battle buddy.
You work, play, laugh, cry, and even get battle-bloody.

This person you would go through battle, fire, or a wall for.
  I would jump off a roof to help my buddy settle a battle-score.

  A battle buddy is like a best friend you choose over all.
You always battle-answer their 2am battle-call.

For your buddy you are always rolling, battle-bowling,
  strolling, patrolling, and even some battle-consoling.

  Their children and family are yours until the battle's ends.

Get a battle buddy and know the true meaning of a battle-best friend.

Relationship Table

Daters, where are you? I know you are out there!
Well listen up, these words are because I care.

What do you bring to the relationship table?
Is your resumé limited and is your life style stable?
Are you living within your means or are you stealing cable?

You want a relationship, but your judgment is unstable.

Here is a good one you may see on any doormat.
Someone would say, "Where are all the good men or women at?"

Basically, they are hiding from you as they search for a qualified mate.

Your credentials are questionable, and you wonder why you can't get a date.

Improve your resumé, get over your issues, solve your problems, and change your attitude before you step to the relationship table.

Then you could attract a serious partner and remove
yourself from that list of people who are un-datable.

You have got to bring something to the table if you want me to stay.

Some just have their hands out and it is not to pray.

They just bring "Wants" to the relationship and nothing of much value.

I can do bad all by myself too and I don't have to feed, carry, or deal with you!

So, improve your credentials, get over your past, and at least bring optimism to the relationship table.

This way your next relationship will have a better foundation and be a lot more stable.

Decision

Today I want you to give me your heart, followed by your mind.
   Then I want your trust and loyalty, along with your behind.

Yes, I want all of you and I know exactly what I am saying.
   See Baby, it's for you that, to God, that I have been praying.

I need a respectable, vulnerable, trustworthy, hard-working queen.
   Stop playing games with my emotions and join this winning team.

Look, I am already successful, Baby. I work hard, and I don't need much motivation.
   My hope is you will join me, and together, we'll make an unbeatable combination.

I need someone to watch my back, while walking beside me. I need you to watch my front as well and, in my absence, I need you to lead.

We are a team and we will make decision together, that is the plan. I am the leader, you're my adviser: I need you to understand.

But make no mistake, I am the man and I have no problem taking care of my part.
   I handle my business daily, so to be my lady, you have to be smart.

First, you have got to know that my love language is "Acts of Service," and when making love with me, you've got to be on your "A" game, no time for acting nervous.

I'm not trying to put you under any pressure or cause you to rush, but as for me, and my house; we will serve God, that is a must.

I have another rule from the Bible I need to tell you before I take my seat. See Baby, in my house, "If you don't work, then you don't eat."

Everyone does his or her part, that's how things work and that's what it is about.

Otherwise, we burden society, and everyone is standing around with their hands out.

If you put your hand out to me, I will fill it today, if that is your wish, but tomorrow, I will give you a pole with some bait and teach you how to fish.

I might also give you some seasoning, some utensils, and a book, because I don't want you to eat that fish raw, it tastes much better when it is cooked.

So, make the decision to join my team as I extend my hand to you.

Become my queen because together there is nothing we cannot do.

All Meat and No Potatoes Inspired by Leslie Slemmons

WOW, her body reminded me of a meal
with all meats and no potatoes,

because with her, there is no room
for vegetables or fruits like tomatoes.

See, her body was so thick
she could stop traffic or ground airplanes

because that body was thicker than
fog from evaporating rain.

She was put together like
a masterpiece, simple, perfection.

Walking by men and causing eight out of ten
of them to get an instant erection,

because heck, the other two of them
were not even paying attention.

The other eight men were held
in compete suspension.

Shaped like a hour glass with multiple
curves beyond simple comprehension.

She was standing right in front of me
but that body was from another dimension.

All meat and no potatoes, well
let me explain what that means

once you finish with the main course
there is no room for green beans.

No youngsters, no beginners, no virgins
or amateurs could ever turn her head.

She needs a full-grown man with his lunch
packed, to satisfy her in bed.

A man needs to be focused, his mind right
and don't come at her like a jerk,

because if you want to make love with her
you will have to put in a lot of work.

Her body is so fierce and so tight
she could set off a dormant volcano.

No matter where she goes, that body
attracts all kinds of Negroes.

When she walks in the room
heads turn like dominoes.

Men and women's eyes survey her body
trying to penetrate her like torpedoes.

Hell, she got my attention, as I
was held captive by her as well.

I had to put my hands in my pockets
just to keep them off her tail.

It is clear she needs a real man to deal
with her mind, body and soul, no zeroes.

That is why I describe her as a woman
who is "All meat and no potatoes"

Lover's Prayer

God, please bless and
protect my heart.
Watch over them when
we are together or apart.

Guide, protect, and
lead them through
all the things
they need to do.

Heavenly Father, please bless
all my family and friends,
and if it is Your will,
forgive us all of our sins.

Bless those who
are in harm's way
Please continue to bless those
who have, from You, strayed.

Bless my enemies, the ones
I know and the ones I know not.
Let them know, I am not here
to fight, love is all I've brought.

Remove any hate from my heart
and anything not pleasing to You.
Order my steps and thanks
for always seeing me through.

Bless those children standing
in the need of prayer.
Bless the elderly so they know
someone actually does care.

Bless those who do not know You
and those who feel out of place.
Keep us all covered by
Your amazing grace,

Your immeasurable love
and Your unbeatable protection
Help us understand, love sometimes
comes in the form of correction.

Thank you for blessing me
with my worldly possessions,
and please forgive me
of any transgressions.

Now as I lay
my head down for rest,
I know with You
my heart is blessed.

If this is the last night
on earth that I see,
please let me wake up
in heaven with Thee.

Acknowledgments

Pre-Sex and After Sex was written with Ms. Creolness

IV

Unseen Romance .... 3 June 2009 (To all the online daters out there)
Second .... 23 April 2016 (Inspired by Life Coach Ivy Allen)
My Queen.............................. 12 August 2009 (Dedicated to Princess)
Hello Again .... 1 August 2009 (Inspired by Yessennia)
A Note to the "I"..................... 27 November 2012 (Inspired by Indihra)
Team Sears............................ 26 November 2012 (Inspired by Indihra)
The I Has It .... 28 November 2012 (Inspired by Indihra)
Apple Pie.............................. 14 April 2016
Vessel .... 13 April 2016
Early Morning Come Back...... (Inspired by Ms. C. Driver 15 April 2016)

V

Biblical Love Poem .... 21 June 2010
Love Story .... 24 April 2012
A Good Thing........................ 28 April 2012 (Dedicated to Mrs. Tawania S-F)
Forgive .... 23 April 2012

VI

Love or Hate? .... 22 April 2016
Rumble (Trust vs. Love) .... 21 April 2014
Love Talk .... 16 March 2011
The Language of Respect ...... 30 April 2016
Battle Buddy................................11 April 2015 (Inspired by Ms. Creolness and the United States Army)
Relationship Table .... 28 April 2016
Decision .... 29 April 2012
All Meat and No Potatoes...... 21 January 2011 (Inspired by my cousin Leslie Slemmons)
Lover's Prayer .... 5 April 2014

Bless you for reading and remember,
Love is Coming for You!

– Mr. Speaker

www.ingramcontent.com/pod-product-compliance
Lightning Source LLC
Chambersburg PA
CBHW031219120626
46545CB00003B/909